DEDICATION

This book is dedicated to all those front rowers who can't find a friend to practise their scrums with outside of training.

"Today I will do what others won't, so tomorrow I can accomplish what others can't." - Jerry Rice

Have the perseverance and initiative to go and get it.

ACKNOWLEDGEMENTS

I would like to acknowledge and thank all of the scrum coaches who have helped in my development as a front rower throughout the years - Andrew Blades (NSW Country Eagles), Cam Blades (NSW Waratahs), Damien Cummins (Warringah Rats), Marco Caputo (Gungahlin Eagles), Chris Hickey (mentor), Mario Ledesma (NSW Waratahs), John Manenti (Eastwood) and Neil Tunnah (Greater Sydney Rams).

In addition to these coaches, there are countless front rowers, both professional and amateur who I have trained with, played against and learned a great deal of scrum knowledge from that I would also like to thank.

There are pieces of advice that I've taken from each of them which, combined with my own experiences, have had a large impact on my game. From specific drills I've needed to practise, through to words of wisdom that come to mind during certain scrummaging situations, it has, and will continue to have a positive influence on not only me, but on all those who read this book.

Most importantly, I would like to thank my family and close friends for always believing in me at times when I may not have believed in myself.

CONTENTS

PART ONE - Analysing the Scrum

PART TWO - Practical Application

PART ONE

Analysing the Scrum

1. INTRODUCTION

 The scrum needs to be broken down into its individual components in order to better analyse and identify problems on the most basic level. There is no point jumping straight into live scrum drills without having a strong foundation in the individual technical aspects of the scrum.

Many individual problems are often attributed to a basic technical error, which is easy to identify and correct in a solo drill before that problem is taken to a live scenario. A lot of teams spend the majority of their preseason packing against a scrum machine or doing live 8v8, without giving enough attention to the individual components that make up that 8 person scrum. It is only once they have had a poor scrum performance that they begin to pick apart where it went wrong, when the problem could have been fixed much earlier on.

Most of the preseason should be spent working on individual weaknesses and developing team cohesion, and then move towards 8v8 drills as the season draws closer. The purpose of this handbook is to equip both players and coaches from any level of the game with the resources needed to build the strongest possible foundations for a dominant scrum.

It covers drills that individuals can complete on their own with little or no equipment, through to eight person drills. Individual scrum drills make up the majority of the drills in this handbook, all of which should be mastered before moving on to more advanced or live scenarios. The many different connections that make up the scrum from each individual are outlined in detail to make the scrum as cohesive as possible.

Common problems that are encountered by the various positions in the scrum are identified. Solutions to these problems are provided for both individual and team feedback, resulting in improved scrum performance.

For players, it offers unique advice on different techniques so that you always feel 'comfortably uncomfortable' at scrum time. It will equip you with the knowledge needed so that all members of your scrum are working together for the same outcome, and no one is off fighting their own battle.

For coaches, use this handbook throughout the season, but with the bulk of the focus during the preseason. Use this to communicate with all players in the scrum when obtaining feedback, so that you can offer solutions to the problems they may be facing.

More often than not, coaches will provide generic scrum advice to their forwards, which can often be misunderstood or misinterpreted. Even specific advice when given verbally, not through actions, can mean very little to a player. Only once a player knows the correct action to change upon understanding your advice will they be able to make a positive difference. The old 'push harder' means nothing when the player is already pushing with 100% effort, but in the wrong manner.

Depending on the various scrum laws of age-based rugby, the principles in this handbook apply, however some exercises may need to be modified to their most simple form.

> Often it is not a big change or adjustment that needs to take place, but in fact only a small change that will make a big difference.

When the scrum machine was locked away and before I could get access to a key, the post with or without a pad served the same purpose. That is why I've put together a collection of the drills that can be practised on your own, and with little to no equipment. Whilst the emphasis of this handbook is on the individual player drills, there are a number of team drills that are explained in detail, with progressions to follow, all of which flow on from the individual drills.

It's these individual skills, that when applied to the entire scrum, great things happen.

> From my own experience, it's often a challenge in itself to find another player, let alone a front rower to practise with.

2. TRANSFER OF FORCE

The front row is the contact point of which force from all eight players is transferred through the opposition. More than 60% of the force is generated from the back five players.

Poor scrummaging mechanics can result in suboptimal power being transferred, weakening your scrum, and in some cases causing injury.

Individually, your hips are the link between your lower and upper body strength, they transfer force through your trunk and shoulders. You need to be in an optimal scrummaging position to effectively and efficiently transfer this force, and this applies to all eight players, not just the front row.

Optimal scrummaging mechanics

The vector of the arrow, particularly of the torso, needs to be flat (or very slightly down) to effectively transfer the force generated from behind you, through the scrum. The height of the scrum needs to stay down and not 'wave' up and down as this releases pressure. Pressure needs to be applied continuously throughout the duration of the scrum. As soon as a players shoulders or hips come up, or they lift a foot during a stalemate, this pressure is released and the opposition will edge forward. All movements must be methodical and coordinated.

The most important player in the scrum is the tighthead prop. If the tighthead goes backwards, the whole scrum goes backwards. It's that simple. By focusing on this principle, the scrum needs to send the weight through the tighthead side, which places a tremendous amount of pressure on the opposing loosehead and hooker. It is essential to this process that the loosehead sends weight through their inside leg and hips whilst still remaining square to avoid being penalised for angling in.

A common theme amongst inexperienced front rowers is that they move away from the weight of the scrum, chasing the 'fools gold' and end up exposing themselves. This is when a player is falsely lured into thinking that they are dominating because it feels 'easy' for a short period of time, until the opposition surges through them.

Players need to work into the weight, not away from the weight. It is much harder to work into the weight, than it is to follow the easy way out and go with it. By going into the weight, you increase the pressure on the opposition, forcing them to go with it, and dismantling their scrum in the process.

3. CONNECTIONS

The goal of the scrum is to apply as much pressure to the opposition, and minimise or eliminate leakages. Leakages of pressure generally occur when one or more of these connections are poor.

When binds are not tight between players (intra-connections), when binds between the front rows have poor biomechanics (inter-connections), and when the connection with the ground is not optimal (external connections).

There are 3 main connections: binds between players, binds to the opposition, and the connection of your feet to the ground.

3.1 Intra-connections

Connections Between Players

1   Loosehead to hooker

Connections of the shoulder and hips are most important. The loosehead binds underneath (behind) the left shoulder of the hooker to create a block for the opposing tighthead. The loosehead needs to keep their right hip connected with the hooker, by driving off their inside leg.

2   Hooker to loosehead and tighthead

Connections with both props are vital to the stability of the scrum. Connection with the loosehead is mentioned above, and it is the hooker's responsibility to ensure the binds are secure. Hookers need to use their shoulders (something many hookers don't know how to do) to keep these connections secure. Hip connections need to be secure with both props to ensure that the back five have a platform to send their weight through.

3   Tighthead to hooker

Connections of the shoulder and hips are most important. The tighthead and hooker should have shoulders next to each other, with the left shoulder of the tighthead slightly promoted in front of the hooker. This connection stops the opposing hooker splitting your hooker and tighthead apart. The tighthead needs to keep their hip connection tight by driving off their inside (left) foot.

4   Locks to loosehead and tighthead props

The locks need to have the point of their shoulder right up the middle of the prop's 'clacker', not wide and low on the back of their hamstring. Locks need to crotch bind onto the shorts (or jersey) of the prop, and wind them down onto their shoulder by pulling their elbow back towards their ribs. This connection cannot weaken or be readjusted on the engagement. Their head needs to be at the same height as their shoulders. Locks need to stay connected with their props at all times, no matter what is happening in other areas of the scrum.

5   Lock to lock

This connection is one of the first to be lost, especially if the hit is lost. Inside shoulders need to remain connected, and minimum weight needs to be applied through the hooker, particularly on your own feed.

6   Flanker to props and locks

Their shoulder needs to be parallel to that of the lock, with pressure applied right through the middle of the prop, and not too wide and low on their hamstring. The bind to the lock doesn't need to be super tight as this may pull them away from their locking partner.

7 No.8 to locks

Both shoulders need to be connected to the locks, up their 'clacker', with their arms securing this connection through their bind on the lock's hips.

3.2 Inter-connections

Binds Between Opposing Front Rows

Every prop will have a preferred way of binding on to their opposite prop. With that said, the most successful props are those who adapt their binding technique to the opposition and are confident with a number of different ways to bind. There are 3 kinds of binds: aggressive, reactive and passive.

> These interconnections are important for both the stability and the strength of the scrum.

An aggressive bind is one that is fast and forceful and aims to unstabilize the opposite prop whilst giving you a strong and stable platform. A reactive bind, is one that can be adjusted on the go if you're on the receiving end of an aggressive bind, and focuses on changing your bind to a stronger one.

> Passive binds cause the most collapsed scrums.

Passive binds shouldn't even be mentioned in this handbook but are important to recognise, as many props tend to use this technique when fatigued. These are the binds with no target in mind, which are not being used to apply any pressure and can be observed most commonly by how slow they are, covering the shortest distance.

Binds need to be seen as a distinct way of showing the opposition what they're in for before the engagement. An aggressive bind puts a little bit of doubt into the opponent's mind and is a great way to apply pressure. Before the engagement, it allows the props to use all the weight behind them and apply it through their opposing props.

Binds also include the head position on the opposing front row. Using a 'lean' on the opposing front row's shoulders (not heads) is a great way to balance the weight from your own scrum, and also allow you a faster opportunity to get your head in the right position on the set, as you have a shorter distance to cover. The lean shouldn't be confused with being pre-engaged as there is still space between the front rows, just a short amount. Simultaneously on the bind and lean, the front row needs to lower their height to the height at which they wish to scrum. Common problems with binds, and their solutions can be found in section four.

3.3 External Connections

Connection With Ground

Foot placement is an ever-changing aspect of scrum time. Whenever there is a new scrum law introduced disruptions to the footing generally occur and modifications need to be made.

Individual differences such as limb length, height, width, etc. mean that 'one size fits all' isn't the case with your feet set-up. Often coaches will give advice in relation to this, but don't take into account the stature of the individual, and how certain cues may be irrelevant or impractical for that player.

The most common example of this is coaches referring to hip and knee angles based on a 'generic player' and having these angles at 110 - 130 degrees. For some players, this advice will work. But what about shorter players and taller players and their differences in lever lengths. Do these angles still mean the same for them? Could a shorter prop be in a more dominant position at angles around 90 - 110 degrees? Absolutely. At 110 degrees a shorter prop will feel very overextended whereas a taller prop may feel cramped.

It might be more appropriate, although very broad, to encourage hip and knee angles of 90 - 130 degrees, based on where the player feels the strongest.

With that said, players don't want to be too wide (no power), or too narrow (no stability or power) with their foot placement, and the direction of their foot in the ground needs to point the way they want to go.

After the set, there should be no foot movement, unless necessary to move forward if you've won the hit. All 16 feet need to be driving the ground away, building pressure. Any foot movement after the set call, even if moving forward creates instability within the scrum. This instability causes a weakness of connections and an inefficient transfer of force. If this occurs, the focus needs to be on rebuilding that pressure as quickly as possible to avoid further disruptions.

4. COMMON INDIVIDUAL PROBLEMS AND THEIR SOLUTIONS

Below are some common problems that occur in each position of the scrum, why they occur and what you can do to fix them:

Front Row

Loosehead Prop

1 Angling in/stepping around the corner - this loses the connection with hooker and doesn't give the lock anything to push on

Keep hips connected to hooker by driving more weight off your inside leg. Make sure that after the set, your first step is always 'forward and in' and off your inside leg. When you make your first step with your outside leg, it opens up the space between your hips leaving you no other option but to chase the angle in.

2 Hunched position with elbow down on bind

The easiest way to correct a hunched posture is to stick your chest out and squeeze your shoulder blades together. This can be accomplished much easier if you use your bind to push the opposing tighthead up and back, which in turn, will flatten your back.

When you pull your elbow down with your bind, you're actually helping the tighthead put more pressure on your neck and back. You're pulling them onto you. Use your bind to your advantage.

3 Not getting your head under tighthead's sternum and sitting outside their armpit

Before you take your crouch position, pick a target on the tighthead's chest, and aim to get your head under it. Try using your head once crouched, to push the tighthead's head in, and this may cause them to readjust their height, giving you an easier target. The lower you get, the easier this becomes, particularly if you're up against a taller opponent.

4 Pulling hooker too far left, away from tighthead

When you pull your hooker towards you, you leave your tighthead scrummaging on their own. Use your connection with the hooker to send your weight to the tighthead by driving off your inside leg.

5 Getting split from hooker - poor shoulder and hip connection

Make sure to communicate with your hooker if they're not driving their left shoulder down onto yours. Again, by keeping your hip connection with the hooker, this will help preserve the integrity of your shoulder connection.

6 Foot position - getting too wide, narrow, over-extended or cramped

This is one of the most common mistakes made by looseheads. Each loosehead is different with the foot placement they prefer. Some like to set up with their left leg forward and then move it back on the bind, others prefer to have both legs already set, either is fine.

Keep in mind that if you set up too wide you wont be able to generate any power from your lower body, and too narrow will make you unstable and powerless. Setting up with your feet too far forward will make you fold in half on the set, and if you survive the hit, your angle of force will make the scrum collapse. You will have no power from a cramped set-up and will be forced to either collapse the scrum, or readjust your feet.

On the other hand, being too over-extended isn't necessarily a bad thing, so long as you can shorten up your steps and readjust into a more powerful position. When you're over-extended, you cannot transfer force effectively, or build pressure because it simply has nowhere to go. You need to bring your feet up slightly, decreasing your knee angle so that you can then drive forward, transferring this force.

7 No weight going through inside leg

Keeping in mind all of the above points, you'll see the importance of driving off your inside leg. Too much weight on your outside leg will weaken your hip and shoulder connection with your hooker and cause you to chase an angle. Conversely, driving through your inside leg will strengthen all of these aspects.

Hooker

1 Set up too high (getting popped)/close/far away from the mark

Every front row will have a preferred and ideal gap from which to set up from. With the current laws, most teams are relying on some form of 'leaning' to gauge an appropriate gap from the opposition. When all front rowers are using their lean and binds to hold the weight and keep the gap, it increases the potential of a powerful and dominant hit. Setting up too far away will cause the scrum to collapse, and setting up too close will likely result in both front rows standing up. If the hooker gets caught too high upon the hit, they are more likely to be popped up.

Practising your set-up to gauge your preferred gap will help build the habits to ensure that you always get your height and spacing right before the set.

2 Getting split from either prop - not using shoulders and/or hips

This is one of the most common problems amongst hookers. They can be too passive at scrum time with their shoulders, and as a result, they weaken and often lose their connections with their props.

The left shoulder, with the force of the loosehead's shoulder combined, needs to bear down and block the space of the opposing tighthead, otherwise a good tighthead will split this connection and destroy your scrum. The right shoulder of the hooker needs to be in line (or fractionally behind) with their tightheads and again, needs to be buried down to block the opposition hooker from getting a 'pincer' on your tighthead.

Hookers must not plane forward with their hips on the set call, as this will lose the hip connections with their props and as a result, the back 5 won't have a stable platform to transfer their weight through.

3 Pulling tighthead in

As mentioned above, the weight of the scrum needs to be heading towards the tighthead. Often when the loosehead steps around the corner, they pull the hooker with them, which has a domino effect on the tighthead, who then also gets pulled sideways. To counter this, the hooker needs to work closely with the loosehead to shift the weight towards the tighthead.

4 Poor strike on ball

Striking the ball is a skill needed by all hookers, but is rarely practised. The current scrum laws make the strike of the ball even more important, and teams often target a hooker with a poor strike once the ball is fed.

Hookers need to work with their halfback on the timing of the feed to coordinate the strike. Hookers need to avoid twisting their hips and shoulders (rotating towards the ball) on the strike as this creates weak connections and a poor transfer of force. This skill can be practised on your own against a scrum machine, single man sled or post.

5 Foot position - getting too wide, narrow, over-extended or cramped

Setting up too wide often gets in the way of your prop's foot position. Being too narrow will result in poor stability once the scrum is set. Your right foot should be viewed as a 'hand-brake' and on the set, you lift the brake to drop the weight and pressure onto the opposition.

On opposition ball, or after the strike, your role is now a third prop, and you must be in a strong position to effectively transfer the force. Being cramped or over-extended will have the same impact as it does on a prop.

Your foot positioning needs to be wide enough to effectively scrum, and also in a position that will allow you create an optimal ankle, knee and hip angle to scrum. Taller vs shorter hookers will need to adapt the same way a prop of the same stature would.

Tighthead Prop

1 Setting up too high - getting popped up

Many tightheads unintentionally raise their height as they reach to get their bind. Lowering your height at this point is the easiest way to prevent getting caught too high. By keeping your right shoulder down and applying pressure to the back of the loosehead's neck, you protect yourself from being opened up. As soon as you lift the height of your shoulder for any reason, a good loosehead will exploit this opportunity, so it's important to maintain pressure through your right shoulder.

This is particularly difficult, especially when your scrum is moving forward. Maintaining your height whilst advancing is crucial to not getting popped up and remaining in control. Your height is closely related to your foot position, and if you get caught too overextended you can start to plane up (like a plane during take off) which exposes your shoulder height.

2 Unintentionally angling in on the opposing hooker

Tightheads with a weak neck can get bullied by a loosehead who pushes their head towards the hooker to make them angle in. It is often the easy way out and away from the pressure for a tighthead to angle in, and frequently rolling in and under the scrum if they cannot control the movement. Although this is a tactic employed by some countries/teams and can have a very dominant effect, more often than not this happens unintentionally.

This is often penalised for angling in if the tighthead manages to keep it up, or penalised for 'cranking' if you roll under.

It is paramount for the tighthead to stay square, and out at the loosehead before trying to chase angles onto the hooker. Only once the tighthead has taken care of the loosehead (job number one), by exposing a weakness, can the tighthead shift the focus to the hooker.

23

Tighthead Prop

3 Foot position - getting too wide, narrow, over-extended or cramped

Getting caught in a cramped or over-extended position exposes you to the 'double edged sword' of collapsing the scrum as you've got no way to transfer the force without moving a foot. But then not moving a foot can result in getting popped up or collapsing if the pressure from the opposition is more than you can generate.

The same principles of foot width that apply to the loosehead's foot position are the same for the tighthead, with a few differences. It is most important for the tighthead to have their feet in the strongest position possible before the set, as moving them after will result in a leak of pressure.

Keeping in mind these principles, whatever foot position allows you to maintain and increase pressure without compromising your scrum, is the best foot position for you.

4 No weight going through inside leg

Similar to that of the loosehead, the tighthead needs to keep weight going through their left (inside) leg to prevent the opposing loosehead and hooker from splitting them. Think of your left leg as a stake in the ground at an angle which is working against the opposing loosehead and hooker - you need to drive it in. If you're putting too much weight through your right (outside) leg, you're weakening the hip and shoulder connection with your hooker, and this will open you up to angling in on the hooker unintentionally.

5 Angling straight down

As mentioned above in relation to set-up height, by keeping the pressure down on the loosehead's neck with your shoulder, you can keep them out of the contest. The angle at which you drive your shoulders down is only a very small amount. Too much downward pressure will look like you're pulling the loosehead down, but going straight on will make you more susceptible to being popped up. It is a fine line, but again, a small change (in angle) can make a big difference to the amount of pressure you make the loosehead endure.

6   Getting split from hooker - poor shoulder connection

This shoulder connection needs to be rock solid. The tighthead can be fractionally in front of the hooker's right shoulder.

If you're too hidden behind your hooker, you're ability to use your left shoulder to apply pressure diminishes, and it can also cause you to roll in, and under the scrum as your left shoulder is much higher than your right shoulder. Aside from your loosehead and hooker not helping you out, you can preserve this connection by not going off on your own against the loosehead if your hooker is not ready/can't.

7   Binding too long and high on opposing loosehead

See previous chapter for more information on binds. Tightheads who use a long bind expose themselves for a loosehead to get underneath them much easier. In order for the tighthead to control the loosehead, they need to control their arm and head through their bind. Using a 'vice grip' technique, the tighthead uses their own head/neck and bind to lock in against the loosehead's head and shoulder and apply pressure. The loosehead cannot do anything to combat this without first leaking pressure for you to expose.

8   Missing the hit

Often you will miss the timing of the hit when you're in an uncomfortable position and are still adjusting after the bind. If this happens, it is still possible to stay in the contest, and even dominate. You need to make any adjustments as quickly as possible after you've missed the hit, in order to get back into your strongest shape. Remember that it is often small adjustments that make a big difference, not a big adjustment.

The best way to avoid missing the hit is to find your position as fast as possible on the bind and be aggressive on the set call.

Second Row

1 Pushing on prop's hamstring, NOT through the middle of their 'clacker' - poor shoulder position on bind

Pushing through the hamstring of the prop will weaken them, and not transfer any force for the scrum. This is the result of a poor shoulder bind. The front of your shoulder needs to be right up through the centre of the props 'clacker' so that power can flow through them in the most efficient manner.

2 Putting too much weight through hooker and not staying with their prop which pushes the prop's hips out, creating angles

By pushing through the hooker, you limit their ability to strike the ball, and put them off balance. When this happens, you effectively pincer the hooker which splits their connection with the props, and as a result creates an angle of the prop's hips and the pressure is dissipated. You need to stick with your prop at all times and ensure your force is transferred through their trunk and not the back of their legs.

3 Getting legs narrow, over-extended/cramped - too much foot movement prior to the feed

The foot positioning principles of the front row are also applicable for locks. The foot position will directly affect the quality of the force transfer through the prop. Too cramped, and the weight will be applied to the prop's hamstring. Too overextended and the weight will drive up the back of the prop, not straight through them. When locks apply pressure, they too must maintain their height so as to not leak pressure before trying to apply it. You'll often see the hip's of the locks go up higher than their shoulders in an attempt to generate power, but as explained above, if their hips get above their shoulders, this power is angled straight down on to the hamstring of the prop. Too much foot movement prior to the feed weakens connections and decreases the stability of the scrum.

Just as the front row need to minimise/eliminate their foot movement prior to the set, so too must the locks stick to these principles. Pressure needs to be applied through the tightening of binds (intra-connections) and through foot positioning (external connections).

4 Falling forward during set-up causing a reset

Whilst this is also a responsibility of the No.8, the locks can also help prevent this from occurring by ensuring their weight is going through the centre of the front row, and not down or up.

Back Row

1 Pushing on props hamstring, NOT through their 'clacker' - poor shoulder position

The same mechanics mentioned above for the locks also applies to the flankers. Force needs to be applied through the centre of the prop through a strong shoulder connection.

2 Losing connection with lock and driving at an angle on the prop

An aerial view of the scrum shows this image the best when the two flankers are both angling in on their respective props, creating an 'arrow' type effect. Flankers must maintain the same force transfer as the locks and props by sending the weight in the same direction, not the opposite. Their heads should be driving the same angle as what their prop is.

3 Leaving scrum too early - worrying about the next job

This is one of the most controversial mistakes that flankers make as they have a very difficult decision to make: do they stay on the scrum, or do they focus on the opposing No.8/halfback/five-eigth? Just as the tighthead prop needs to take care of his opposing loosehead before focusing on the hooker, so too must the flankers do their primary job at scrum time first.

If your scrum is under pressure 5m out from your own line, your sole focus needs to be adding as much weight as possible. Once the scrum is done, then you can worry about your other roles. When you leave the scrum early and pop your head up to see the status of the ball, you release pressure from the prop and it's at this time during the scrum that a pushover against you is imminent. Scrum first, worry about ball second.

Conversely, when it is your scrum that has dominance, this allows you the freedom to potentially leave early and get about doing your other jobs.

Flankers

4 Not communicating during own and opposition feed to coordinate actions

Most of the scrum doesn't know where the ball is once it's been fed. It is for this reason that flankers need to communicate with the scrum to coordinate actions. By making a call when the ball has been fed, the rest of the scrum can react accordingly so as to ensure a strong platform is given on your own feed, and to disrupt the opposition feed as much as possible.

No.8

1 Adding no weight to the back of the scrum - poor shoulder position and over-extended

This can be associated with the attitude of the player. Is the scrum a chance for a rest, or a chance to apply as much force as possible? The same strong shape with foot positioning and hip and shoulder height needs to be achieved to apply as much force through the locks, whilst also keeping the integrity of the shoulder connection to help keep the locks together. No.8's need to hold the weight of the locks back until the "set" call to ensure there is no early transfer of force resulting in a pre-engage.

2 Leaving scrum too early and popping up head to look around while the ball is still in scrum - worrying about next job

This is the same as it is for flankers, only when you leave early, the entire scrum suffers as there is no longer someone at the base of the scrum keeping all the connections together. Stay on the scrum.

3 Poor dribbling skills at base of scrum when going forward resulting in a knock on or turnover

The worst thing you do can as a No.8 is to lose control of the ball (whether it be your feet or hands) on the way to a pushover try. This skill is very rarely trained, yet can have such a positive impact on the scrum when done successfully. Practicing on a single man sled is the best way to improve this vital technique.

5.COMMON TEAM PROBLEMS AND THEIR SOLUTIONS

Below are some common problems that occur with many team's scrum, why they occur and what you can do to fix them:

Problem:

Moving forward before the ball is fed and giving away a free kick.

Likely cause:

It could be a couple of things. Firstly, the hooker may be setting too far forward and not leaving much space for themselves or their props to get an optimal lean on the opposition. Secondly, the back 5 might not be holding their weight back during the set-up causing the front row to fall forward.

Solution:

In the first instance, the front row need to practise their set-up with their ideal gap, and make sure that the opposition isn't closing their space. If it is the back five falling forward, work needs to be done with the No.8 on holding the weight back, as well as improving the height of their shoulder connection to the prop.

The scrum going back and reshuffling immediately after the hit (different to missing the hit). It looks like a front row issue, but often it's not. When you look at it closely, it often comes across as a recoil like action where the scrum gets parody or even wins the hit, but then gets pushed back as soon as the opposition builds pressure.

Likely cause:

There are two main causes of this, and it can be a cause and effect.

The hooker may be 'losing their hips' on the set (planing forward like a plane during take off) which results in no weight being transferred from the back 5 through the front row.

If this isn't the case, then the back 5 aren't giving enough weight to the front row. This is the more likely scenario.

Solution:

The hooker needs to practise (by themselves initially) setting against a single man sled or scrum machine until they can keep their hips up on impact. They then need to work through the front row drills (see part two) and achieve the same outcome - no hip plane.

For the weight transfer, you need to work on the connections between locks and props in a 2v2 scenario, as well as the connections from the entire back five. See the drills later for a more in depth explanation.

Problem:

Stepping around the corner - loosehead prop wheeling the scrum.

Likely cause:

Loosehead prop is looking for an easier way to attack.

Solution:

Make sure your loosehead prop is keeping their hip connection to the hooker and driving off their inside (right) leg. Their first step needs to be into the weight. See individual problems chapter, which outlines this in more detail.

If you encounter an opposition who wheels the scrum, use these principles to send weight through your tighthead, which will exploit the opposing loosehead even further.

Too much movement after the bind call.

It could be a number of different causes. Primarily, when the opposing prop has an aggressive bind, it can put the affected prop off balance, causing them to make last minute adjustments, which disrupts the rest of the scrum.

Another potential factor could be that your tighthead is already heading in on an angle, and sending their weight across the scrum, making your loosehead unbalanced and feeling like they're getting pushed out of the scrum.

Lastly, the connections from the back five may be the reason for last minute adjustments to be made. Too much readjusting from behind puts doubt in the mind of the front row before they set.

Props need to be more aggressive with their binds and use them to transfer the weight coming from your scrum through your opposing prop.

As a loosehead, you need to talk to your tighthead and hooker and make sure they're sending their weight onto the opposing loosehead and hooker respectively. Looseheads also need to ensure that they're sending the weight through their inside leg and hooker on the set-up, and this will put them in a more comfortable and stable position without any balance problems.

If front rowers are feeling uncomfortable during the set-up, stand up and talk to the back five about what they're doing, and how they can fix it. Prevention is better than intervention from the referee.

6. SCRUM SET-UP

The hooker should be viewed as the leader of the scrum, and they set the gap and the height of your scrum.

Every time a scrum is packed it needs to follow the same process. This process must remain the same, so that when new players come onto the field, or into the team, the performance of the scrum is not disrupted. The following steps offer a basic outline as to how the scrum should be set up.

1. Loosehead binds first.

2. Tighthead binds second.

3. Front row set.

4. Locks bind in and hold weight. Locks need to be careful not to open up the space between the hips of the hooker and props as the extra space will weaken this connection. Locks can start with one knee down, or both knees down, but both locks must be doing the same thing.

5. Flankers bind on and need to be careful not to unbalance the props or locks (some props prefer the flanker to hold them back too).

6. No.8 binds on and holds weight.

7. Hooker calls front row down.

Referee: "crouch, bind, set"!

* Front rowers see set-up drills for further detail.

PART TWO

Practical Application

Mastering the three levels of any drill is critical to the overall development of your scrummaging. Don't put the cart before the horse. Master level one, before moving onto the next drill. Habits that you form during these initial drills, in particular, will stick with you (whether they're good or bad), so it's important that you focus on improving from the ground up.

Videoing yourself, even just with your phone, provides immediate and valuable feedback as to how you are progressing. The footage never lies. Sometimes you think you are ready to move to the next drill, but the footage shows otherwise. Be honest, disciplined and patient with your progress. You are not going to improve overnight, but consistency and repetition is guaranteed to improve your performance.

SCRUM HACK: understand the above before starting any drills.

7. SCRUM DRILLS AND SEASON PLAN

> When your scrum is under pressure and adjustments need to be made, it's important to get back in the strongest position as soon as possible.

These drills are not the only scrum drills that you can do. They do however, develop the fundamental skills that need to be understood and applied if players are to progress their scrummaging to an elite level.

Each exercise builds upon the previous one, whilst adding an extra layer of knowledge and skill to it, culminating in the player mastering their own strongest position.

Individual drills	1. All forwards		
	2. Front row		
Live scenario drills	3. 1v1 - All forwards	7.	3v3 - All forwards
	4. 1v1 - Front row	8.	3v3 - Front row
	5. 2v1 - Front row	9.	5v5 - Tight 5
	6. 2v2 - Tight 5	10.	8v8 - All forwards
Season plan	8 week preseason scrum training program		

7.1. Individual Scrum Drills - All Forwards

At some point you're going to be on the receiving end of a dominant scrum. That's ok. The purpose of these drills is to not only provide a dominant platform at scrum time through strong foundations, but also to ensure that the right countermeasures are in place so that if things go wrong, they can be corrected simply, and rapidly.

All drills have two levels that can be completed with little to no equipment, and a third progression, level three, that requires a partner to assist.

The purpose of the base position drills is to ensure that no matter what internal or external pressures are experienced at scrum time, all players can maintain a strong position, or get back into a strong position once they've become unstable.

Every player in the scrum needs to be able to demonstrate a solid foundation in all three of the 'base position drills' before progressing to any 1v1 drills.

Whilst some drills already have a ball incorporated, it can be used in any of the drills. By placing a ball on the mid-back and trying to keep it there throughout the drill, you can add another level of difficulty. It is also a great feedback tool for identifying weaknesses/leakages of energy. Ensure the ball is pumped up.

You should always maintain a strong position.

Base Position - Static

This is the foundation movement that all future drills are based off.

This is the most basic of all the movements and it focuses on your body awareness and how you respond to being in an unstable position. All three levels of this drill form the foundations upon which all other drills are built on, which is maintaining your strongest position.

1. Start by kneeling down with hands on ground, just in front of your shoulders and at shoulder width apart.

2. Come up onto your toes, with four points of contact with the ground (both hands and both feet). Your feet should be just wider than your hips, and your head should be in a neutral position, looking forward 1m in front of you. Your back needs to be flat and parallel to the ground and with hip and knee angles of 90 - 130 degrees (this will vary with each player).

3. Breathe into your diaphragm to brace your core as you push your weight into your 4 points of contact.

4. Maintain a strong position and overcome any external pressures with careful focus on not overcorrecting movements.

Level one	• Hold position for 15 seconds • Repeat x 5 reps
Level two	• Lift hand and foot off the ground, hold for 3 seconds • Repeat x 3 reps each side • Repeat x 3 sets
Level three	Partner required; same as level 1 but your partner is trying to unstabilize you by applying constant pressure alternating between the head, neck, shoulders, arms, torso, hips, knees and ankles. *The amount of pressure applied is dependent upon the player's ability to maintain the shape of level one.

Keep your hips and shoulders level (not rotating/tilting) when lifting your hand and foot off the ground, or when external pressures are applied.

Base position static   Level 1 - holding shape

Base position static   Level 2 - alternate hand/foot lift

41

Base Position - Dynamic

You'll now start to introduce some movement. Always keep your hips and shoulders down when introducing movement into your scrummaging drills. Taking a big step for example, shifts the height of your hips which then changes the direction of force that's being transferred. As a result, your shoulders will either go up or down (the opposite of what your hips do) and if the scrum doesn't collapse, you won't be in a position to dominate. Often players will find themselves over correcting their movement, putting them into an even worse position than before. Small movements make the biggest differences.

1. Set up four cones in a 1 metre x 1 metre grid.

2. Get into the *base position.*

3. Move forward 1 metre and back 1 metre with your alternate hand and foot moving simultaneously. These are small movements; your hands and feet should only just come off the ground.

4. Next, move left 1 metre and right 1 metre with your alternate hand and foot moving simultaneously.

   Move your inside leg first (widening your foot base) at the same time you move your outside hand (narrowing your hand base). *Inside leg is the direction you are going.*

   Then move your outside leg in to recreate the base position. At the same time, you move your other hand out to recreate the base position. Being too narrow makes you unstable, and being too wide gives you no power.

5. The cue for foot placement is "wide to base, wide to base". With hands being simultaneously opposite "close to base, close to base".

Level one	• Move forward/back 1m, then left/right 1m = 1 set • Repeat x 3 sets
Level two	Same as level 1, with ball on back x 3 sets
Level three	Partner required; same as level 1 with a resistance band/rope around your waist with your partner trying to pull you in different directions. If no equipment is available, your partner is trying to unstabilize you as in *base position static level 3.*

Keep hips down when moving.

42

Base position dynamic   Level 1 - forward and back , left and right

Base position dynamic   Level 2 - same as level 1 but with ball

Base Position - Around Grid

The same principles from the *base position - dynamic* apply here. Co-ordination under fatigue is the focus of this drill. It's very easy to become 'sloppy' with your technique once fatigue sets in, and this is where the habits you've created from the previous 2 drills will start to show.

1. Set up four cones in a 1 metre x 1 metre grid.

2. Get into the *base position.*

3. Move around the grid; clockwise direction. Utilise the same movements from the *base position - dynamic*, focusing on keeping your actions synchronised whilst moving.

Maintain a strong position and overcome any external pressures with careful focus on not over correcting movements.

Level one	• 1 lap around grid • Repeat x 3 sets
Level two	Same as level 1 but with ball on back x 3 sets
Level three	Partner required; same as level 1 with a resistance band/ rope around your waist with your partner trying to pull you in different directions. If no equipment is available, your partner is trying to unstabilize you as in *base position dynamic level 3.*

Movements are synchronised and methodical. This is not about the speed at which you complete the grid; it's about the quality of the movements.

Base position around grid
Level 1 - no ball

Base position around grid
Level 2 - with ball

7.2. Individual Scrum Drills - Front Row

The set-up responds best to repetition. The more you do it, the better you'll become, and the more it will come naturally without necessarily thinking about it during the game.

A few reps a week aren't enough to change your habits. You need to prioritise your time to developing your routine through hundreds and thousands of reps during the preseason, and then maintaining the quality of reps during the season.

Quality is paramount, but you can also incorporate the right quantities to ensure you're making the most of your time. There's no need to reinvent the wheel. Look at what the best in the world do. You may need to tweak things slightly as everyone is different.

Players need to know their own role technically at scrum time before moving on to live scenarios.

Find a world-class player with a similar stature/physique and see what works for them.

Create new habits and awareness when you're under pressure.

Set-up Routine with Band/Harness/Rope

Your set-up routine is one of the most important processes that you need to go through prior to, and during a scrum. A generic example would be:

- As soon as a scrum is called, you flick the switch - this triggers in your mind everything you need to do to have a dominant scrum. It starts from you approaching the scrum.

- Know where you are going to bind onto your team mate/s. Take your bind. Get feet and shoulders in the right position.

- Open your chest, squeezing your shoulder blades together, and brace your trunk.

- Pick your hit target on your opposition.

- Follow the referee call ("crouch" - crouch, "bind" - bind on opposition and sink, "set" - win the hit). Make necessary adjustments.

Every player will have their own unique set-up routine that makes them feel the most comfortable. Creating a set-up routine is all about creating/changing habits. Once you've trialled a few different set-ups, you'll find one that works best for you. After that, it's about following this process every single time you set up for a scrum. Developing your routine takes time, but will soon become second nature.

1. Secure band, harness or rope to an anchor point and loop the other end of it around your waistline.

2. Walk forward, away from the anchor point until there is enough tension to prevent you from falling forward.

3. Go through your entire set-up routine including the referee's call.

Level one	• Hold for 15 seconds • Repeat x 10 reps
Level two	• Sink and pulse for 15 seconds • Repeat x 10 sets
Level three	Props only: bind with band and pulse for 10 seconds x 10 sets *You will need an additional band

 Work hard to find the position you feel the strongest in.

47

Set-up routine   Level 1 - hold

Set-up routine   Level 2 - sink and pulse

48

Set Up and Hit Against Single Man Scrum Sled/Scrum Machine/Post with Pad

The set up and hit drill is similar to the set-up routine, except this time you're going to work up to an engagement, which is the primary focus, but your set-up process will remain exactly the same.

Speed, intent and focus is what you need to 'win the hit'. If you win the race for space during the engagement, you've taken a huge step to winning the scrum.

The most important thing to keep in mind during this drill is to maintain your technique. You need to remain in a strong position as you make contact with the post or machine.

1. Follow set-up routine.

2. For level 2 and above, incorporate the "set" call, or hit, into the routine and engage into the apparatus.

3. Build pressure through the apparatus and chase feet into a strong position if necessary when using a sled or scrum machine.

PROP

Level one	Crouch, bind and sink x 25 reps
Level two	Crouch, bind and sink, hit x 25 reps
Level three	Crouch, bind and sink, hit, build pressure for 5 seconds x 25 reps

HOOKER

Level one	Crouch and get correct spacing x 25 reps
Level two	Crouch and hit x 25 reps
Level three	Crouch, hit, build pressure for 5 seconds x 25 reps
Level four	Same as level 3 without the 5 second pressure build, but this time you will focus on your ball strike x 10 reps

Lower your height after/at the same time as your bind, and maintain a strong position throughout the entire exercise.

Hookers on level 4 need to keep their shoulders level and not twisted when striking the ball (you will need to work on the flexibility of your hips, glutes and hamstrings).

LIVE SCENARIO DRILLS

You will notice that the majority of the drills in this section follow the same exercises and level progressions. They are a progression of the individual drills done previously, and follow the same principles.

As you move through the different scenarios, additional players are introduced, bringing with them, new challenges and different connections to focus on.

For the purposes of all these drills, a *'fold in'* scenario involves getting into the final position of a scrum, without the actual engagement.

7.3. 1v1 - All Forwards

- ○ Prop vs prop
- ○ Hooker vs hooker
- ○ Lock vs lock
- ○ Back row vs back row

During all these drills NO hands are to be on the ground, and your head needs to be under the chest of your opposition, NOT sitting outside their armpit.

All members of the scrum need to be proficient in these 1v1 drills as they form the foundations of which all other drills will be built upon.

Drills can be made more difficult by placing a ball on the mid-back and trying to keep it there throughout the movement. It is also a great feedback tool for identifying weaknesses/leakages of energy.

Base Position - Static : 1v1

Focus on getting under your partner's chest as this will allow the best transfer of force, as opposed to sitting out under each other's armpit, where the force is dissipated. Work together so that both players can get equal benefit. It's important that you give each other feedback during this initial drill, as you want to correct any bad habits before progressing.

1. Set up opposite each other in your base position.

2. Fold into your set-up with both heads under the chest, and one bind (the side your opponent's head is under) and apply pressure to each other as you come up off your knees. Take your other bind once you are both stable.

3. Start level one once both players are in this position.

4. Level 2 requires the same set up, but this time, both players are lowering and raising the height of their hips and shoulders by sinking down with their knees and chest. It only needs to be a small movement, as you want to preserve your position. Do not move your feet.

5. Level 3 allows one player to build pressure while the other absorbs. Similar to level 2, these are not large movements. Again, don't move your feet, but move your hips forward into an extended position (not over-extended) whilst building pressure. Hold for 3 seconds. Now it's your partner's turn to build pressure. When you absorb the pressure, your hips will be pushed back, but not into a cramped position - think like a slingshot getting loaded.

Level one	• Hold for 30 seconds • Repeat x 4 sets
Level two	• Pulse for 15 seconds • Repeat x 6 sets
Level three	• Build and absorb pressure x 3 reps = 1 set (1 rep = both sides having built and absorbed pressure) • Repeat x 3 sets

Keep your binds up (not pulling down) and elbows up. The more you pull your elbow down, the more pressure you're putting on your own neck and upper back. Keep your shoulders level and not tilted/twisted to either side.

Base Position - Dynamic : 1v1

Both players need to work together to complete the drill correctly. Be mindful not to pull your partner down onto your neck (elbow down and shoulders rounded is the giveaway), and that you're both generating equal amounts of resistance so that neither of you get overextended or cramped. The onset of fatigue during this drill is much earlier compared to the individual drill.

One player will be the leader, and the other will follow their movements. E.g. if the leader moves forward, the follower moves back and vice versa.

1. Set up four cones in a 1 metre x 1 metre grid.

2. Get into the *base position - static 1v1,* but this time move forward/ back with small steps. Remembering the same principles from the individual base position dynamic drill.

3. Level 2 involves moving laterally. Remember your foot placement of "wide to base, wide to base" to ensure you don't get caught too narrow and unstable. It's important to stay square and in front of your opponent when moving laterally, to keep the transfer of force going in the same direction.

4. Level 3 is where it gets tough, and when your legs start to burn. This is the same as the individual base position around the grid, only this time you have an opponent in front of you. You need to work together during this drill, and focus on keeping your binds up, and your foot movements in sync.

Level one	• Move forward/back 1m • Repeat x 5 sets
Level two	• Move left/right 1m • Repeat x 5 sets
Level three	• 1 lap around 1m x 1m grid • Repeat x 3 sets

Keep hips and shoulders level and not tilting/ twisting with each movement. Work hard on staying in front of your opponent, so that you don't allow them to take an angle on you.

7.4. 1v1 - Front Row

Set-up

The same as the individual set-up drills, but now you'll put those habits into practise against an opponent and work on your inter-connections (connections with opposition).

Being able to get instant feedback from your bind and lean is a great way to practise what seems to be working for you, whilst also trialling some different methods. It will also help you develop great habits around your spacing and foot placement, and how that relates to your engagement, as well as what happens after.

1. Set up opposite each other with enough space so you can both go through your set-up routine.

2. For level 1, both crouch, bind and lean onto each other (use imaginary bind with other front row on your team), and sink. Do everything except the set.

3. For level 2, go through all of the above, this time, incorporating the set call and hold your strong position for 5 seconds.

Level one	• Crouch, bind (lean and sink) • Repeat x 15 reps
Level two	• Crouch, bind (lean and sink), set and hold for 5 seconds • Repeat x 15 reps

Don't get caught too high on your set-up. Sink lower as you find your bind and lean.

7.5. 2v1 - Front Row

These drills are the same as the 1v1 drills for all forwards, however this time you are adding in another front rower which adds an extra level of difficulty.

Base Position - Static : 2v1

This is the first drill for the front row that works on the intra-connections. The pair of players needs to focus on keeping their hip and shoulder connection together, whilst the player on their own is trying to bury their way through those connections.

1. Set up opposite each other as you did in the *level 1 base position - static 1v1 drill.*

2. Start level 1 once all three players are in position.

3. Level 2 follows the same principles as *level 2 base position static 1v1 drill,* however the pair of players needs to focus on keeping their hip and shoulder connections tight. The player on their own needs to work hard to maintain a strong position despite the added pressure.

4. Level 3 follows the same principles as the *level 3 base position static 1v1 drill.* Focus on keeping the height of your hips and shoulders down as you build and absorb pressure.

Level one	• Hold for 30 seconds x 2 reps = 1 set • Rotate players between sets • Complete x 3 sets total (each player does 4 reps in the pair, 2 reps as the individual)
Level two	• Pulse for 15 seconds x 2 reps = 1 set • Rotate players between sets • Complete x 3 sets total (each player does 4 reps in the pair, 2 reps as the individual)
Level three	• Build and absorb pressure x 3 reps = 1 set (1 rep = both sides having built and absorbed pressure) • Rotate players between sets • Repeat x 3 sets total (each player does 4 reps in the pair, 2 reps as the individual)

Keep your binds and elbows up (not pulling down). The more you pull your elbow down, the more pressure you put on your own neck and upper back. You also want to focus on keeping your shoulders level and not tilted/ twisted to either side.

Base Position - Dynamic : 2v1

When movement starts, players take angles and work away from the weight, instead of into it. Staying square and in front of your opposition is the most important aspect of this drill. When you stay in front of the weight, you can transfer force more efficiently than you can if you were to work towards the outside, which loses your connections in the process.

One group will be the leader, and the other will follow their movements. E.g. if the leader/s move forward, the follower/s move back.

1. Set up four cones in a 1 metre x 1 metre grid.

2. Set up the same as the *level 1 base position - dynamic 1v1*. Move forward/back with small, synchronised steps.

3. Level 2 involves moving laterally, the same as *level 2 base position dynamic 1v1*. Remember your foot placement of "wide to base, wide to base" to ensure you don't get caught too narrow and unstable.

4. Level 3 is the same as the *level 3 base position - dynamic 1v1*, only this time you have more weight in front or beside you. You need to work together during this drill, and focus on keeping your binds up, and your foot movements in sync. It can get tricky during this stage, so it's important to remain focused on what you're trying to achieve.

Level one	• Move forward/back 1m x 2 reps = 1 set • Rotate players between sets • Repeat x 3 sets total (each player does 4 reps in the pair, 2 reps as the individual)
Level two	• Move left/right 1m x 2 reps = 1 set • Rotate players between sets • Repeat x 3 sets total (each player does 4 reps in the pair, 2 reps as the individual)
Level three	• Move 1 lap around grid = 1 set • Rotate players between sets • Repeat x 3 sets total (each player does 2 reps in the pair, 1 as the individual

Whilst moving around, the front row needs to maintain a strong stable platform through their hips and shoulders.

Set-up : 2v1

Building up from the 1v1 set-up, the focus remains the same, but with an added emphasis on getting your head and shoulders in the right position, and at the right height. Have a target that you're focusing on hitting.

1. Set up opposite each other with enough space so you can both go through your set-up routine.

2. For level 1, all crouch, bind and lean onto each other, and sink. Do everything except the set. The added weight in front or beside you will make this more difficult.

3. For level 2, go through all of the above, this time, incorporating the set call and hold your strong position for 5 seconds. The pair need to focus on keeping their hip and shoulder connections whilst the individual needs to focus on keeping hips and shoulders down.

Level one	• Crouch, bind (lean and sink) • Repeat x 15 reps
Level two	• Crouch, bind (lean and sink), set and hold for 5 seconds • Repeat x 15 reps

Don't caught too high on your set-up. Sink as your find your bind and lean.

7.6. 2v2 - Tight 5

To a certain degree, a prop is only as good as the lock behind them. These drills teach the importance of the shoulder connection from the lock, and how the direction of force transfer impacts the prop's ability to transfer it. Props need to give feedback to their lock continuously and tell them when they feel they're in the strongest position possible.

 The front row needs to feel the weight and support coming from behind, whilst the locks need to have a strong platform for which to transfer this force.

Base Position - Static : 2v2

This is one of, if not, the most neglected scrum drill - the connection of the locks to their props. Despite players and coaches talking about "sending the weight through", it's an area that is often forgotten. And for this reason, there are many props who may have been 'better scrummagers' had they had a lock behind them who was taught how to 'send the weight'.

1. Set up opposite each other in your two pairs, as you did in the *level 1 base position - static 1v1* drill. Locks bind with the point of their shoulder right up the 'clacker' of the front rower. Front rowers need to give locks feedback at this point to ensure they have the support they need.

2. Start level 1 once all 4 players are in this position.

3. Level 2 follows the same principles as *level 2 base position - static 1v1* drill. Locks need to focus on moving in sync and keeping their shoulder connection with the prop.

4. Level 3 follows the same principles as *level 3 base position static 1v1 drill*. Both locks need to focus on keeping constant pressure going through their prop. Props need to give feedback to their locks about the positioning of the lock's shoulder particularly when building pressure.

Level one	• Hold for 20 seconds • Repeat x 4 sets
Level two	• Pulse for 10 seconds • Repeat x 6 sets
Level three	• Build and absorb pressure x 3 reps = 1 set (1 rep = both sides having built and absorbed pressure) • Repeat x 3 sets

The front row needs to feel the weight and support coming from behind, whilst the locks need to have a strong platform for which to transfer this force. Maintaining the height of the shoulders and hips is crucial during this drill.

Base Position - Dynamic : 2v2

This drill focuses on the transfer of force once there's some movement from any direction. Once movement becomes one of the variables, the pack who can maintain their connections and stay square and in front of the weight the longest/most efficiently will come out on top.

Locks talk about not knowing what to do if their prop gets spilt from the hooker - always stay with your prop. As a lock, you need to transfer the weight through your prop, whilst also strengthening their connection with the hooker. Maintaining constant pressure is the biggest challenge of this drill, but it can be overcome by staying in front of your opponent and focusing on small movements.

One pair will be the leader, and the other will follow their movements.

1. Set up four cones in a 1 metre x 1 metre grid.

2. Set up the same as the *level 1 base position - static 2v2.*

3. Start level 1 once all four players are in position. Move forward/back with small, synchronised steps. Focus on keeping constant pressure.

4. Level 2 involves moving laterally. Remember your foot placement of "wide to base" to ensure you don't get caught too narrow and unstable. The front row need to stay in front of their opponent, whilst the locks need to stay square, to keep the transfer of force going in the same direction.

5. Level 3 is the same as *level 3 base position - dynamic 1v1*, now with more weight behind you. Work together, and focus on keeping your binds up, and your foot movements in sync. It's easy to switch off and lose coordination once fatigue sets in, so remain focused.

Level one	• Move forward/back 1m • Repeat x 5 sets
Level two	• Move left/right 1m • Repeat x 5 sets
Level three	• 1 lap around grid • Repeat x 2 sets

The front row needs to maintain a strong, stable platform through their hips and shoulders for the locks to transfer force.

Set-up : 2v2

Incorporating the set gives great insight into the strength of the shoulder connection from the lock during the impact of the set. From the team problems in part one, the strength or weakness of this connection is highlighted on the engagement. A strong connection means the prop won't move, and a weak connection means the prop will recoil after the set, despite potentially winning the hit.

The previous drill focuses on maintaining constant pressure, and this element will be exposed after the set, if it's not occurring.

1. Set up opposite each other with enough space so you can go through your set-up routine that same as the *1v1 front row set-up.*

2. Locks bind with the point of their shoulder right up the 'clacker' of the front rower.

3. For level 1, both pairs crouch, bind and lean onto each other and sink. Do everything but the set. The props should feel 'loaded up' from the weight of the locks behind them. Locks need to ensure that their weight is being transferred through the centre of the prop, otherwise it can cause them to pre-engage.

4. Go through all of the above, this time, incorporating the set call and holding your position for 5 seconds. Focus on building constant pressure straight after the engagement and make sure that the integrity of all connections are maintained.

Level one	• Crouch, bind (lean and sink) • Repeat x 15 reps
Level two	• Crouch, bind (lean and sink), set and hold for 5 seconds • Repeat x 15 reps

Keep the connections between front row and lock. Constant pressure needs to be applied from the locks so that there is no rebound/recoil after the set.

Prop (loosehead preferably), hooker, lock
vs
Prop (tighthead preferably), lock, flanker

Transfer of force efficiently from the back five members, through the front row. This means staying square, and keeping constant pressure.

Base Position - Static : 3v3

Building upon the foundations that have already been laid, we now add more weight to the equation. You can start to work on the different combinations of players during this drill in a more position specific way. For the front rowers, this adds other elements to front row specific 2v1 drills done earlier on.

1. Set up opposite each other in your groups, as you did in the *level 1 base position - static 2v2 drill.* The front row should feel 'locked in' and very stable.

2. Start level 1 once all six players are in this position.

3. Level 2 follows the same principles as *level 2 base position - static 2v2 drill.* Both groups need to ensure that they are transferring the force efficiently through strong connections and in the right direction.

4. Level 3 follows the same principles as *level 3 base position static 2v2 drill.* Locks and flankers need to focus on keeping constant pressure and minimising any unnecessary movements. Props need to give feedback to their locks and flankers about the positioning of their shoulders particularly when building pressure.

Level one	• Hold for 15 seconds • Repeat x 4 sets
Level two	• Pulse for 10 seconds • Repeat x 6 sets
Level three	• Build and absorb pressure x 3 reps = 1 set (1 rep = both sides having built and absorbed pressure) • Repeat x 3 sets

The front row needs to feel the weight and support coming from behind, whilst the locks and flankers need to have a strong platform for which to transfer this force. Maintaining the height of the shoulders and hips is crucial during this drill.

Base Position - Dynamic : 3v3

Adding in the element of movement starts to show the quality of all the intra and inter-connections. All six members need to work together to get the timing and coordination right.

One group will be the leader, and the other will follow their movements.

1. Set up four cones in a 1 metre x 1 metre grid.

2. Set up the same as the *level 1 base position - static 2v2*.

3. Start level 1 once all six players are in this position. Move forward/back with small, synchronised steps.

4. Level 2 involves moving left/right. Remember your foot placement of "wide to base". Locks and flankers need to keep connections with the front row. The front row will work to stay square and in front of their opposition, in order to give the locks and back row the best platform to scrum from.

5. Level 3 is the same as *level 3 base position - dynamic 2v2*, now with more weight behind and beside you. This is one of the most challenging of all the base position dynamic drills. Each player focuses on their core role in order for the group to move efficiently. As with all the drills, focus on the quality of the movement, not the speed at which you can complete it.

Level one	• Move forward/back 1m • Repeat x 5 sets
Level two	• Move left/right 1m • Repeat x 5 sets
Level three	• 1 lap around grid • Repeat x 2 sets

The front row need to maintain a strong stable platform through their hips and shoulders for the locks and flankers to transfer force.

Set-up : 3v3

The added weight of this drill gives the front row more confidence in the players behind or beside them, whilst also providing more stability. This extra weight provides an additional challenge, particularly to the front row, as they now need to send more weight through their binds, on to their opponent, who then has to absorb it.

1. Set up opposite each other with enough space so you can go through your set-up routine that same as the *2v2 set-up*.

2. For level 1, both groups crouch, bind and lean onto each other and sink. Do everything but the set. The props should feel 'loaded up' from the weight of the player/s behind them. Locks need to ensure that their weight is being transferred through the centre of the prop, otherwise it can cause them to pre-engage. Flankers need to remain square and driving in the same direction as their prop.

3. For level 2, go through all of the above, this time, incorporating the set call and holding your position for 5 seconds. Focus on building constant pressure straight after the engagement and make sure that the integrity of all connections are maintained.

Level one	• Crouch, bind (lean and sink) • Repeat x 10 reps
Level two	• Crouch, bind (lean and sink), set and hold for 5 seconds • Repeat x 10 reps

Keep the connections between front row, lock and flanker. Constant pressure needs to be applied from behind so that there is no rebound/recoil after the set. All players need to be sending weight in the same direction.

7.8. 3v3 - Front Row

These drills work on the hip and shoulder connections, as well as promoting the front row to work as one.
You can place a ball between the hips of the props and hooker, with the goal of keeping it there. This highlights the integrity of the hip connection.

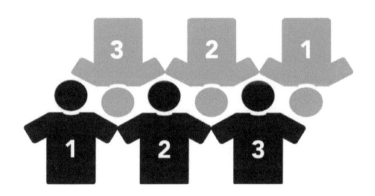

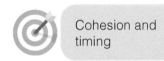

Cohesion and timing

Base Position - Static : 3v3 Front Row

This is the first drill that involves all three front rowers working together on the same team.

1. Set up opposite each other as you did in the *level 1 base position - static 2v1 front row drill.*

2. Start level 1 once all six players are in this strong position.

3. Level 2 follows the same principles as *level 2 base position - static 2v1 front row drill*, this time the numbers are even on each side. Focus on lowering your hips and shoulders, by sinking with your knees and chest as you squeeze your binds together.

4. Level 3 follows the same principles as *level 3 base position static 2v1 front row drill.* Keep your hip and shoulder connections. As you build pressure focus on sending the weight through to your tighthead. It's important to maintain a strong position as you absorb pressure so you can efficiently transfer the force back when it's your turn to build pressure.

Level one	• Hold for 15 seconds • Repeat x 4 sets
Level two	• Pulse for 10 seconds • Repeat x 6 sets
Level three	• Build and absorb pressure x 3 reps = 1 set (1 rep = both sides having built and absorbed pressure) • Complete x 3 sets

The front row needs to have strong connections between their shoulders and hips.

Base Position - Dynamic : 3v3 Front Row

This is the final movement of the base position dynamic series. It's most challenging, both physically and mentally and requires you to push your boundaries. Coordinating the timing of foot movement is one of the biggest obstacles of this drill. It is dependent on the stature of the players involved and can vary from group to group.

One group will be the leader, and the other will follow their movements.

1. Set up four cones in a 1 metre x 1 metre grid.

2. Set up the same as the *level 1 base position dynamic 2v1 front row drill*. Move forward/back with small, synchronised steps. Maintain the height of your hips and shoulders as you move forward and back.

3. Level 2 involves moving left/right the same as *level 2 base position dynamic 2v1 front row drill*. Remember your foot placement of "wide to base" to ensure you don't get caught too narrow and unstable. Your foot placement can become very tricky, so focus on your coordination and timing, rather than your pace.

4. Level 3 is the same as the *level 3 base position dynamic 2v1 front row drill*, only this time you have more weight in front and beside you. Use your binds to your advantage and don't pull your opposite prop down onto your neck. Stay square and in front of your opponent to keep hip and shoulder connections intact.

Level one	• Move forward/back 1m • Repeat x 5 sets
Level two	• Move left/right 1m • Repeat x 5 sets
Level three	• 1 lap around grid • Repeat x 2 sets

Focus on all the principles you have learned; height, connections and foot placement.

Set-up : 3v3 Front Row

This is the first official front row engagement. All the drills in the lead up to this set-up have put you in a great position to see how much you've improved. It's an opportunity to work on different combinations, as well as familiarising players with their spacing and set-up routines.

1. Both front rows set up opposite each other with enough space so you can go through your set-up routine.

2. Level 1 is the same as the previous set-up drills. This time you have the entire front row involved. Focus on sinking together as you get your binds.

3. Level 2 is the same as the previous set-up drills. Focus on the hit speed and the hip and shoulder connections upon the engagement.

Level one	• Crouch, bind (lean and sink) • Repeat x 10 reps
Level two	• Crouch, bind (lean and sink), set and hold for 5 seconds • Repeat x 10 reps

The front row need to focus on keeping their hip and shoulder connections after the engagement, and not getting split apart.

Foot Strike : 3v3 Front Row

Striking the ball is a skill that hookers need to work on individually, in addition to the team environment. Timing the strike with the feed is something that hookers need to work on with the halfback. Practising this drill highlights the quality of the hooker's position during the strike. It's important that hookers keep their shoulders and hips at the same height, without twisting, as this can open up the space needed for the opposing front row to exploit.

The focus is on the hooker's scrummaging position and connections during the strike, and the quality of the strike. Markers can be placed in various positions behind the loosehead's feet to practise striking through to various targets.

1. Both front rows fold in to the set-up

2. Once there is a stable platform, feed the ball in on the hooker's signal, and strike it back between the loosehead's feet. Maintain the pressure, despite not having a full engagement.

3. Level 1, each team has 5 strikes, rest, and then repeat with the opposition's feed.

4. Level 2 uses the scrum call of "crouch, bind, set" to engage the scrum. Everything else remains the same.

Level one	• Fold in for the set-up • First hooker x 5 strikes • Rest • Second hooker x 5 strikes • Repeat x 2 sets
Level two	• Crouch, bind, and set • First hooker x 5 strikes • Rest • Second hooker x 5 strikes • Repeat x 2 sets

Hooker needs to get a clean strike on the ball whilst not twisting through their upper body, which loosens the shoulder and hip connections with the props.

7.9. 5v5 - Tight 5

The tight 5 are the engine room of the scrum. Connections and communication between these five players are critical to having a dominant scrum.

Pressure Build : 5v5

Building pressure is the primary focus of a scrum. Pressure can be built by ensuring that all players have strong connections with all three elements (intra-connections, inter-connections, and external connections), whilst also being in their strongest position with an optimal angle to transfer the force.

1. Follow the scrum call - "crouch, bind, set".

2. Once there is a stable platform, begin to increase the pressure by tightening your binds and sinking lower into the scrum lowering your shoulders and knees. This is essentially a static hold, similar to the *level 1 base position - static 3v3.*

Level one	• 15 second pressure build • Repeat x 5 sets
Level two	• 20 second pressure build • Repeat x 4 sets
Level three	• 30 seconds pressure build • Repeat x 3 sets

Don't raise the height of your hips and shoulders in an attempt to build more pressure. This wave like motion releases the pressure as you go up, which gives the opposition an opportunity to edge forward.

Foot Strike : 5v5

Adding more weight to the equation means that any weakness in connections, particularly from the hooker will be more readily exposed. Hookers can practise the accuracy of their strike with the additional bodies behind the front row.

1. Follow the scrum call - "crouch, bind, set".

2. Once there is a stable platform, feed the ball in on the hooker's signal, and strike it back between the loosehead's feet. It's important that the loosehead lock doesn't get their feet too wide as this can interfere with the striking of the ball.

3. Level 1, one team has 3 strikes, rest, and then repeat with the opposition's feed.

4. Level 2, one team has 5 strikes, rest, and then repeat with the opposition's feed.

Level one	• First hooker x 3 strikes • Rest • Second hooker 2 x 3 strikes • Repeat x 2 sets
Level two	• First hooker 1 x 5 strikes • Rest • Second hooker 2 x 5 strikes • Repeat x 2 sets

Hooker needs to get a clean strike on the ball whilst not twisting through their upper body, which loosens the shoulder and hip connections with the props. On defensive scrums (opposition feed), coordinate the pressure to increase as the hooker raises their leg to strike the ball.

7.10. 8v8 - All Forwards

There is no magical number for the amount of scrums that should be packed in an 8v8, or 8 vs machine scenario. What's important is that the focus is on quality reps.

You also need to consider what else is being done in the session, the training and playing load of the players, as well as what the focus of the scrum session is. All these factors will influence the number of scrums you will pack in a session.

These drills give the No.8 an opportunity to work on their connections and involvement in the scrum.

8v8 - Live Scrum

This is where all the individual components practised previously can come together in a successful formula.

There are number of different things you can practise in a live 8v8 scenario:

- O Timing of hit speed
- O Connections (all types)
- O Tactics (props angling in, tighthead standing up, hooker not using their shoulders, etc.)
- O Coordinating pressure as the opposition feeds the ball
- O Locking down and staying square on your own ball and disrupting the opposition ball as much as possible

8v8 live scrummaging is the best way to improve your scrum throughout the course of a season. The more reps players pack together, the more successful your scrum will be.

Whilst this method is the most important for developing team cohesion, it's also the most physically taxing on the body and mind, and quality is always preferred over quantity, especially during the season. You would be better off doing five high quality scrums, than doing 10 scrums of poor quality.

8v8 - Scrum Machine

The vast majority of the drills in this handbook are based on live/semi-live scenarios as these provide the most realistic results at scrum time. Despite its limitations, we can get some benefits from the scrum machine, aside from the individual and front row set up routines.

Firstly, it provides a stable and predictable environment where the team can work on the timing and cohesion of their set. And secondly, it's very useful for identifying potential leakages of force through the various connections.

You can work on these two aspects during live scenarios, but the machine offers a less aggressive avenue to practise these components, and is a great alternative during a deload week.

7.11. Coaching Plan - 8 Weeks

This is ideal for a preseason block of training with a focus on one to two 30 - 45 minute sessions. These aren't necessarily official team sessions, as players should be doing extra sessions in their own time. These drills should form the foundations of your scrum conditioning sessions.

It's recommended to find/assign a partner of the same position for which you can complete extra drills with.

During the season, aside from any problem solving, the vast majority of your scrum time needs to be in a live scenario, focusing on developing/overcoming threats for upcoming opposition.

Use the exercise regressions from the previous weeks as warm up drills for your current training focus. E.g. use the 1v1 drills as warm ups for the 3v3 drills.

WEEK 1   **INDIVIDUAL SHAPE**
                                                        All forwards

- Base position static - level 1, 2, 3
- Base position dynamic - level 1, 2, 3
  Front row also go through their individual set up routine with a band/ harness

---

WEEK 2   **INDIVIDUAL SHAPE**
                                                        All forwards

- Base position around grid - level 1, 2, 3
  Front row also go through their individual set up routine with a band/ harness, and the set up and hit against a machine/sled.

WEEK 3   **1v1**
                                                        All forwards

- Base position static - level 1, 2, 3
- Base position dynamic - level 1, 2, 3
  Front row also go through their 1v1 set up

WEEK 4   **2v2**

(Front row and lock v front row and lock) Tight 5

- Base position static - level 1, 2, 3
- Base position dynamic - level 1, 2, 3
  Front row also go through their 2v1 set up

WEEK 5   **3v3**

(Prop, hooker, lock v prop, lock, flanker) All forwards

- Base position static - level 1, 2, 3
- Base position dynamic - level 1, 2, 3
  Front row also go through their 3v3 set up

WEEK 6   **5v5**

Tight 5

- Pressure build
- Foot strike
  Front row also go through 3v3 set up

WEEK 7   **8v8**

All forwards

- Machine
- Live
  Front row also go through 3v3 set up

WEEK 8   **8v8**

All forwards

- Machine
- Live
  Front row also go through 3v3 set up

8. NECK CONDITIONING

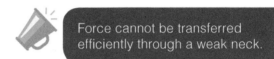

Force cannot be transferred efficiently through a weak neck.

Neck strength is generally the weakest link for scrums and contact, particularly in front rowers. Lower and upper body strength is rarely an issue for these players.

A strong neck is not only important for safety reasons, but it can also be used to get on top of your opponent. Having a stronger neck can reduce the severity and symptoms of concussion from heavy impacts to the head.

All of these exercises need to be done with full core activation (glutes engaged, neutral pelvis, diaphragm breathing). The focus is on maintaining the correct position throughout the exercise whilst under pressure from external forces.

NOTE: You can progress these exercises even further once you have mastered this program. Firstly, you can increase the resistance e.g. amount of weight you use, or the strength of the band. Secondly, you can keep the resistance the same but increase the duration or number of reps of the exercise.

Neck Rotations

For these exercises, your eyes and neck move in the same direction.
Lay on ground or bench with your head slightly lifted off the surface.
The arrows indicate the direction you will move:

- ○ Left ear to left shoulder, right ear to right shoulder = 1 rep
- ○ Forward flexion - chin to chest, back to neutral = 1 rep
- ○ Rotation - turn left, turn right = 1 rep

Level one	25 reps of each x 2 sets
Level two	25 reps of each x 3 sets
Level three	50 reps of each x 1 set

Ear to shoulder — All levels

Bring chin to chest - eyes look up, eyes look down   All levels

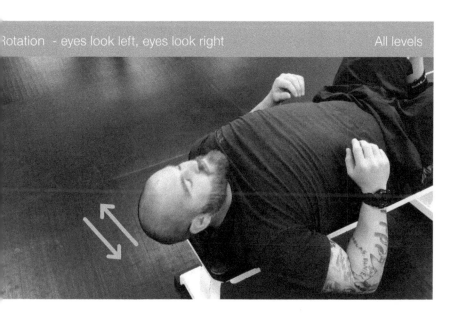

Rotation - eyes look left, eyes look right   All levels

4-Way Neck Hold with Band/Wall/Partner (Neck Plank)

- ○ **Wall/partner:** Keeping your torso upright, lean at an angle against the apparatus using your neck (imagine you are a flat plank of wood - no curves or bends). If with a partner, they push against your head to provide resistance.

- ○ **Band:** Tie band around an anchor point just below eye level. Put band around your head and step away until you reach the correct resistance.

Maintain a strong, braced position throughout.

Level one	Left/right side - 10 second hold x 3 sets
Level two	Left/right side and front - 10 second hold x 3 sets
Level three	Left/right side, front and back - 10 second hold x 3 sets

Band/wall : side   Level 1

86

Band/wall : back   All levels

Forward and Side Flexion

Set up kettlebell/s at the end of a bench with a resistance band looped through the handles.

- ○ **Forward flexion:** Lay face up with your knees on the bench, core activated, and the band around your head, just above your eyes and at the top of your ears. Bring your chin to your chest, without taking your shoulders off the bench.

- ○ **Side flexion left/right:** Lay on your side with your knees bent, core activated, and the band around your head, just above your eyes and at the top of your ears. Bring your ear to your shoulder, then back to neutral, without taking your shoulders off the bench.

Don't let the band pull your head below neutral.

Level one	15 second isometric hold - forward, left and right x 3 sets
Level two	10 reps - forward, left and right x 3 sets
Level three	5 reps with a 3 second hold at the top - forward, left and right Repeat x 3 sets

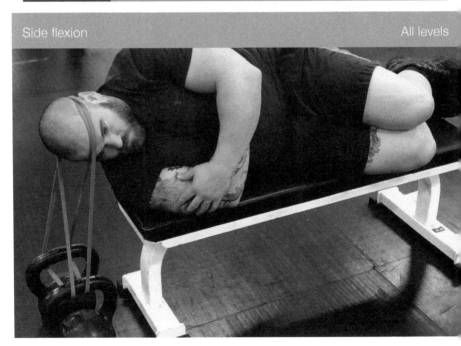

Side flexion   All levels

Neck Extension with Harness or Band

For safety, this exercise should have a coach or parental supervision for players under the age of 15.

○ Set up a barbell in the squat rack at a height that mimics your shoulders at scrum time.

○ Ideally this exercise is done with a neck harness with added weight. Start light and build from there, don't go too heavy straight away.

○ For isometric holds - maintain a neutral head position, with a slight extension, with your eyes looking 1 metre in front of you.

○ For reps - same position as above, but bring chin towards chest just below neutral, but not touching. Then extend back up to just above neutral. It should be a very small movement.

Level one	15 second isometric hold x 3 sets
Level two	15 reps x 3 sets
Level three	15 second isometric hold - 3 points of contact x 4 reps Change lifted point of contact every rep Repeat x 3 sets

Neck extension with harness   Level 1 and 2

Lateral Band Hold

- ○ Loop a resistance band around an anchor point at just above knee height.
- ○ Get into the *base position* and put the band around your head, just above your ears, perpendicular to the anchor point. Shuffle out until there is tension on the band. Increase resistance if needed by moving further away from the anchor point.

Don't let the band pull you left and right. Stay square.

Level one	15 second isometric hold - 4 points of contact Repeat x 3 sets each side
Level two	15 second isometric hold - 3 points of contact x 4 reps Change lifted point of contact every rep Change side of resistance band Repeat x 2 sets each side
Level three	15 second isometric hold - 2 points of contact (alternate hand/foot) x 2 reps Change side of resistance band Repeat x 2 sets each side

Lateral band hold   Level 1 - 4 points of contact

ertical Band Hold

○ Loop a resistance band around an overhead anchor point

○ Get into the *base position* and put the band around your forehead, just above eyes. Don't let the band pull your head up; make adjustments to the height of the anchor point, or the resistance of the band if needed.

Level one	15 second isometric hold - 4 points of contact x 3 sets
Level two	15 second isometric hold - 3 points of contact x 4 reps Change lifted point of contact every rep Repeat x 2 sets
Level three	15 second isometric hold - 2 points of contact (alternate foot/hand each rep) x 2 reps Repeat x 3 sets

ertical band hold   Level 1 - 4 points of contact

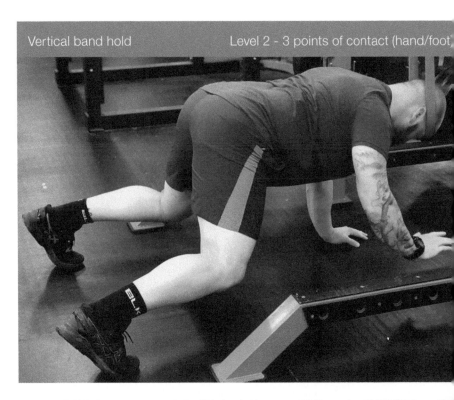

Neck Bridge

- Use a sturdy bench or put bench/chair against a wall or other secure frame.

- Sit on the ground with your knees bent and feet flat on the floor. Lean back so that your head is flat on the bench, with the edge of the bench just above the base of your neck.

- Drive through your heels and lift your hips up, using your neck as the third point of contact to support you. Your shoulders shouldn't be supporting your weight on the bench.

Level one	10 second isometric hold x 3 sets
Level two	10 reps with a 2 second hold at top x 3 sets
Level three	10 second isometric hold each leg x 3 sets

Neck bridge   Level 1 and 2

98

Neck Conditioning Plan - 8 weeks

This program is ideal for a preseason block of training with two to three sessions per week needed in order to get through the plan below. These don't have to be official team sessions, as players should be doing extra sessions on their own in order to complete. Try to complete all levels of one exercise per week.

You can repeat this program throughout the season. Keep in mind that the progressions of each exercise still need to be adhered to, however the order of exercises isn't as important as it is doing the program for the initial 8 weeks.

This could be done before scrum sessions as part of your warm up, or as part of your strength and conditioning program in the gym or at home.

WEEK	EXERCISE/S
Week 1	Neck Rotations
Week 2	4-Way Neck Hold (Neck Plank)
Week 3	Neck rotations and 4-Way Neck Hold
Week 4	Forward Flexion, Side Flexion
Week 5	Neck Extension with Harness/Band
Week 6	Lateral Band Hold
Week 7	Vertical Band Hold
Week 8	Neck Bridge

9. SUMMARY

Roles and Responsibilities

- **Loosehead** - send weight towards the tighthead prop and stay square
- **Hooker** - use shoulders and hips to keep integrity of connections and set the height
- **Tighthead** - win the hit, stay out at opposition loosehead and maintain pressure
- **Locks** - transfer the force in the most efficient way through the centre of the props
- **Flankers** - stay on the scrum until the ball is won
- **No.8** - provide weight and stability to the locks and control the ball at the back of the scrum

Each team will vary with the level of quality of their players and so some teams/players may need to spend more time getting the fundamentals mastered before moving on.

As mentioned throughout this handbook, the onus is on the players to have the discipline to practise a lot of the exercises on their own. However, coaches can use this to form the foundations of their scrum training from the first session of the preseason.

Feedforward and Feedback

It's paramount for the development of your scrum that players and coaches are honest with one another in their feedback. Often it may come across as a personal attack on a player when they've made a mistake, but so long as the criticism is given in a constructive manner, and the player knows what they need to do to fix it, then egos must be left in the locker room if the team is to improve.

If you're practicing on your own, a phone works perfectly well and allows you the ease of seeing movements frame by frame.

Using video footage is a great way to analyse what's happening at scrum time, and provides the perfect opportunity for players to do a self-analysis on their performance. In addition to video analysis, coaches and players should have constructive and proactive feedforward previews of what they wish to achieve during each session and game, as well as feedback reviews post sessions and games.

When previewing an opponent's scrum, look for the common mistakes identified throughout the handbook and have a strategy for how you're going to exploit them. Every scrum will always play to their strengths; so it's important that you identify what you need to do to nullify their threats, but also how you're going to deploy some threats of your own.

Often scrums will become depowered and less dominant when reserves come on the field, so coaches need to ensure that all members of their squad have a solid foundation in these scrum principles, so that through injury or substitution, their scrum remains the same.

This handbook gives you the tools you need as either a player or coach to effectively transform your scrum into a dominant weapon.

ABOUT THE AUTHOR

Samuel Needs is an Australian professional rugby union player who plays in the front row, predominantly as a tighthead prop. He has played for the NSW Waratahs, NSW Country Eagles, Warringah Rats, Eastwood Rugby Club, and is currently playing in Japan.

Away from rugby, Sam is a qualified Exercise and Sports Scientist with over 10 years' experience in the industry. In conjunction with learnings from his strength and conditioning coaches, Sam utilises this knowledge in his own training, so that he

Photo credit: Karen Watso

can develop the necessary optimal qualities needed for his position.

Sam grew up playing rugby for his local team, the South West Rock Gaolers, on the mid north coast of New South Wales. He attended S Joseph's College, Hunters Hill, where he frustratingly was never able to brea into the first or second XV teams. After completing high school in 2008, San moved to Canberra the following year where he continued his rugby journe with the Gungahlin Eagles for three seasons, where he also represented th ACT U20's for two years. Seeking further rugby opportunities Sam returne to Sydney to play in the Shute Shield for Eastwood Rugby Club. Suffering significant ankle injury, requiring two operations, kept him out of rugby fo the better part of two years, and upon returning to the field, he found himsel playing in the lower grades again.

Nearly ready to give the game away, Sam made the choice to persever with rugby, but this time committing himself at a different level to what h had done before, this included many hours of individual scrum sessions, individual gym and field sessions and endless personal sacrifices. It was during this time, Sam realised that it's a challenge to find a regular training partner, let alone another front rower to practise with. Improvisation for scrum specific drills that could be done on his own, and with little to no equipment is how he overcame this obstacle.

In 2015 an opportunity presented itself to play first grade for Eastwood. He won the Shute Shield with Eastwood that year and earned a National Rugby Championship (NRC) contract with the now defunct, Greater Sydney Rams. He moved to the NSW Country Eagles the following year, where they were grand finalists.

In 2017 Sam made his debut for the NSW Waratahs. Following his NRC coach and rugby mentor Darren Coleman, Sam moved clubs to play for the Warringah Rats in the Shute Shield. The Rats went on to win the Premiership that year, giving Sam two premierships at two different clubs within three years.

At the end of the 2017 season, Sam signed to play in the 2018 Japan Top Challenge League.

Photo credit: Ko Iijima